Applied Psychology

Volume 7

PROCESSES AND PERSONALITY

Being the Seventh of a Series of Twelve Volumes on the Applications of Psychology to the Problems of Personal and Business Efficiency

BY

WARREN HILTON, A.B., L.L.B.

FOUNDER OF THE SOCIETY OF APPLIED PSYCHOLOGY

ISSUED UNDER THE AUSPICES OF

THE LITERARY DIGEST.

FOR

The Society of Applied Psychology

NEW YORK AND LONDON

1919

1914

BY THE APPLIED PSYCHOLOGY PRES

SAN FRANCISCO

Republished from the public domain by

Creative English Publishing

www.Creative-English-Institute.com

Under Classic Reads

May 2014

**ISBN-13:
978-1499582529**

**ISBN-10:
1499582528**

Processes and Personality

CONTENTS

WHAT THE EMPLOYEE MUST DO

FOUR INJUNCTIONS FOR BUSINESS CONDUCT

Processes and Personality

NORMAL PROCESSES OF DISSOCIATION

Chapter I

NORMAL PROCESSES OF DISSOCIATION

Classes of Experience

You have learned that Dissociation is a mental principle and process complementary to Association. Just as Association binds together the facts of experience into groups and complexes, so Dissociation selects for immediate emphasis and attention certain groups, certain ideas, certain elements, and causes others to be ignored so completely as apparently to be discarded altogether.

Those seemingly discarded are not Classes of permanently lost. They are merely thrust aside as of no immediate interest or consequence.

In brief, all the facts of experience fall into one or the other of two broad classes: first, those that are active in the present momentary state of consciousness; second, those that are inactive and subconscious.

And this latter class may again be subdivided into two classes: first, those that are ordinarily capable of voluntary recall; second, those that are as a rule beyond reach.

There is no hard-and-fast line to be drawn between these various divisions. They melt into one another by imperceptible degrees. They even change from day to day.

Some facts of experience are for a time so active as to be continually thrust forward into consciousness, even against our will, so that we "can think of nothing else," but within a week we cannot for the life of us remember what they were. A popular air gets to "running through our heads," and for a day we sing it, we hum it, we whistle it, until our friends are no more tired of hearing it than we are, and in a week we try to recall the name of the song and it has slipped our memory.

Other experiences are so closely bound up with our present interest and activities that we can call them forth at any moment without appreciable effort. Still others come "to mind" — that is, to our consciousness — only with hard "thinking". Many utterly defy our efforts to recall them at all.

And beyond all there is a limitless volume of sense-impressions to which we have never given even a passing thought, which we have never even perceived when they occurred, of which we have never at any time been conscious, which would perhaps fail of recognition, even if recalled, which would seem to us a sort of mysterious forecast rather than a memory, and yet which constitute altogether by far the greater part of our experiential life.

We want you to do more than merely grasp the sense of these paragraphs. We want you to comprehend their present significance to you; We want you to feel, to know, that your mind is this vast and complex mechanism. We want you to picture to yourself your mind at this moment as the repository of all your past experience.

Basis of Classification

Just what facts of experience shall be dissociated and shunted off into inactivity and forgetfulness, what ones shall receive some slight passing notice, and what ones shall be emphasized and dwelt upon in consciousness to the exclusion of all else — all this is determined by Interest and Attention.

The Dial of Attention

Now, attention may be conscious or un-conscious; it may be voluntary or involuntary. It is regulated not so much by the will, as commonly understood, as by desire, conscious or unconscious. It is the creature of self-interest. Whatever is related to your interest in life, as you see it, receives your attention. Whatever receives your attention is emphasized while in consciousness, and is afterwards kept close at hand in sub consciousness ready for use.

Desire, interest, and will, then, set the dial of attention. Attention sounds the gong that marks certain elements of experience for special emphasis. Meanwhile the myriad other facts of experience not so particularly designated are dissociated from the important ones and busily stored away in less convenient archives.

Processes and Personality

PATHOLOGICAL EVIDENCES OF SUBCON- SCIOUSNESS

Chapter II
PATHOLOGICAL EVIDENCES OF SUBCON- SCIOUSNESS

Abnormal Dissociation

THERE are many conditions in which this process of dissociation goes beyond the limit of what is normal — that is, it goes beyond the mere setting aside of those things that are irrelevant to our present interests.

When such excessive dissociative activity occurs, it results in the sidetracking from consciousness of sensory material that should be available for our present use. Dissociative activity "run wild" is known as abnormal dissociation.

Hysteric Anesthesia

An abnormal dissociative activity is the most characteristic feature of mental diseases. Anesthesia, for example, is a frequent symptom in persons afflicted with extreme hysteria — that is, there is an apparent loss of sensibility in one or more parts of the body. When this anesthesia occurs the process of dissociation has been abnormal. It has removed from the patient's consciousness sensory impressions that rightfully belong there.

Thus, some spot on the surface of the body may appear insensible to touch or pin-pricks, or even burning. The anesthesia may apply to any of the other organs of sense. The sense of hearing may be lost, or taste or smell. One or both eyes may be blind. Any one or more of these defects may appear, and yet the general health of the sufferer may apparently be undisturbed.

One of the first things that a psychologist does who is investigating a case of this sort is to test the sense-organs of sight, feeling, taste, hearing, and so on, as the condition of these functions has much to do with the state of mind of the subject. Thus, the deafness of one or both ears and the susceptibility of the subject to musical sounds, as shown by ringing a tuning-fork close to the ear, are important parts of the diagnosis.

Now, the startling fact for us in these cases is
that the sufferer actually feels perceives and
remembers sensations without being conscious
of it.

Experiments of Doctor Prince

For example, the hysteric may be afflicted with total blindness and may stare about him with dull, unseeing eyes, yet if he be hypnotized the visual images of all the objects that he has been unable to see will be found to be remembered, showing that the retina and the optic nerve, the sense of sight, has all along performed its full duty, but that the sensations resulting were dissociated from consciousness.

A characteristic instance of this is recorded by Dr. Morton Prince in "The Dissociation of a Personality," as follows :

"Mrs. E. B. met with an accident, and as a result had a complete hysterical anesthesia of the hand. The skin could be severely pinched and pricked without any sensation resulting. Under proper precautions, I pricked with a pin the hand several times, then laid gently upon it a pair of small nippers with flat surfaces and pinched the skin with the same. She did not feel the pricks of the pin, nor did she know that anything had been done to her hand. She was then hypnotized. While in the trance I asked her, —

'What did I do to your hand ?'

'You pricked it.'

'How many times?'

'A good many times, more than twelve.'

'Where did I prick it? Show me.'

Patient indicated correctly with her finger the part that had been pricked.

'What else did I do?'

'You laid something on it.'

'What?'

'Something long and flat.'

'What else did I do?'

'Pinched it.'

'With what?'

'Something you had in your hand; I don't know what it was.'

"The patient was then awakened, and the experiment repeated with variations. After being again hypnotized she was asked what had been done.

'You pricked my hand.'

'How many times?'

'Eighteen.'

'All at once?'

'No; first five times, then thirteen.'

'What else was done?'
'You pinched it.'

'How many times?'

'Five.'

'What did I pinch it with?'

'Your fingers.'

REMEMBERING THE UNPERCEIVED

"These answers were all correct." We want you to notice two features in this experiment. First, you will observe that all these pinchings of the anesthetic hand, which were unnoticed by the patient in a normal state of mind, were remembered by her when she was in the hypnotic trance; secondly, that these occurrences were remembered and were recounted with absolute accuracy.

If you should be possessed with that absurd delusion that hypnotism involves any element of thought transference, brush that cobweb from your mind. When the proper time comes we shall give you a clear and scientific account and explanation of the phenomena of hypnotism. For the present it is enough to say that a hypnotized person is not bewitched, is not asleep, but only in a state of concentrated attention.

EXPERIMENTS OF JANET AND BINET

The experiments of Janet and Binet, distinguished French scientists, have shown that in these hysterical cases the sense-impressions are actually received and are retained in a sub-consciousness that can be "tapped and made to testify to its existence in various ways."

One method of "tapping this subconsciousness" makes use of the customary inability of these hysterics to give attention to more than one thing or one person at a time — a fact which in itself indicates that while the senses may operate in their usual mechanical fashion, the field of consciousness is restricted.

Thus, speaking of one of his subjects, M. Janet says: "When Lucie is talking directly with any person she is no longer able to hear anyone else. You may stand behind her, call her by name, shout abuse into her ears, without making her turn around ; or place yourself before her, show her objects, touch her, etc., without attracting her notice. When finally she becomes aware of you, she thinks you have just come into the room again and greets you accordingly."

Now, with this person, and others like her, it has been found that if one step quietly up behind them while they are absorbed in conversation with some one else and whisper in their ear telling them to do some simple thing, such as to lift the hand to the face or make some uncouth gesture, they will do as they are directed and their talking consciousness will be unaware of the fact.

MEANING OF "AUTOMATIC WRITING"

Going further, by placing paper and pencil before them, they can be made to reply in writing to any simple whispered questions that may be asked, while still animatedly engaged in conversation with the other person and apparently unaware of what the hand is doing. Each manifestation of consciousness, the talking consciousness and the writing consciousness, seems equally unaware of the doings of the other. This sort of "automatic writing," as it is called, is a striking proof of mental activities of which we are unconscious.

The hand of one of these persons, though he will tell you that it is incapable of feeling, will nevertheless adapt itself to whatever object may be surreptitiously placed there. It will open and shut a pair of scissors; it will make movements with a pencil, as if writing, etc.

DISSOCIATION BY HYPNOTIC SUGGESTION

Similar phenomena can be made to order by means of hypnotism. The result will be a process exactly the reverse of what we have been describing.

In the hypnotic state the operator may produce anesthesia by suggesting to the subject that he is insensible in one respect or another. The subject will then be entirely unaware of any sensations that are in conflict with the hypnotic suggestion of the operator. Yet if advised that after awakening he is to give a full account of all that occurred to him while hypnotized, he will do so, indicating that the mind has made a subconscious record of the facts. We shall give the details of an actual experiment of this kind.

The subject, a woman, was hypnotized. The operator then told her that when she should open her eyes she would be unable to see him.

Having made these suggestions, he then placed a hat upon his head. She insisted that it was suspended in the air. She was informed that she was unable to see his glasses, and when he moved them about she followed them with her eyes, but insisted that they were not there.

He placed a newspaper before her, and, taking his suggestion, she saw neither it nor the hand that held it; yet when his finger pointed to certain words she was quick to pronounce them one after the other. When the paper was taken away, she did not remember having seen it nor know what she had been saying about it.

On awakening at the end of this series of experiments, the subject had no recollection of what had occurred. She was then asked to shut her eyes, and a pen was given her. She was told to try to recollect what had occurred when she was asleep. But she could not remember anything. The pen meanwhile wrote without her knowledge an account of what had occurred.

MEMORY LAPSES

It is evident from this that sensations that were apparently not perceived, and so never active in consciousness, were nevertheless unconsciously preserved. Later, through the agency of automatic writing, they were reproduced.

The dissociation of sensory impressions is analogous to an abnormal degree of dissociation in the reproductive processes of memory. In the latter case it tends to place beyond recall certain experiences that the individual needs in his daily life — that is, certain experiences of his past life, or part of it, are dissociated from memory.

THE ANSEL BOURNE CASE

An interesting example of this is the celebrated Ansel Bourne case, reported for the Society of Psychical Research by Dr. Richard Hodgson.

Ansel Bourne was a preacher of Greene, Rhode Island. He disappeared on the morning of January 17, 1887, after having drawn $551 from the bank.

Bourne's disappearance caused a great deal of excitement in the town on account of the money that he had with him. His picture and description were published far and wide. Foul play being suspected, the police took an active part in the search, but no trace of his whereabouts could be found.

On the morning of March 14th, two months later, a man in Morristown, Pennsylvania, woke up in fright and called upon the people of the house to tell him where he was. He declared that his name was Ansel Bourne, and that he lived in Greene, Rhode Island.

The people thought he was crazy. All they knew about him was that he had been calling himself A. L. Brown since his first appearance in Morristown, which was about six weeks previous. He had rented a small store there at that time, stocked it with stationery, confectionery, fruit and small articles. He had never in any way seemed unnatural or eccentric. But now he was declaring that he knew nothing of Morristown, that his name was not Brown, and that he had never owned any kind of a store, and that the last thing he did the day before was to draw some money from the bank in Greene and pay some bills.

Thinking him insane, the people sent for the authorities. Dr. Louis R. Read, who was called in, was also, for a time, The under the impression that the man had lost his mind. However, a telegram was sent to Providence, and Bourne's nephew, Mr. Andrew Harris, arrived on the scene, identified his uncle, made everything straight and took him home.

Bourne was in an extremely weakened condition, having lost twenty pounds. He was horrified when he was told that he had been keeping a candy-store and refused to have anything to do with it.

He had absolutely no memory, after he had once resumed his normal personality, of anything or anyone connected with that interval of two months. His last memory previous to his waking up was of having drawn money from the bank, paying some bills and boarding a Pawtucket horse-car.

In 1890, Professor William James induced Bourne to submit to hypnotism. The result was narrated as follows by Professor James:

"I induced Mr. Bourne to submit to hypnotism, so as to see whether in the hypnotic trance, his 'Brown' memory would not come back; it did so with surprising readiness; so much so that it seemed quite impossible to make him whilst in the hypnotic state remember any of the facts of his normal life. He had heard of Ansel Bourne, but ' didn't know as he had ever met the man.' When confronted with Mrs. Bourne he said that he had never seen the woman before,' etc. On the other hand, he told of his peregrinations during the last The fortnight, and gave all sorts of details about the Morristown episode. The whole thing was prosaic enough and the Brown personality seems to be nothing but a rather shrunken, dejected and amnestic extract of Mr. Bourne himself — during the trance he looks old, the corners of his mouth are drawn down, his voice is slow and weak, and he sits screening his eyes and vainly trying to remember what lay before and after the two months of the Brown experience. 'I'm all hedged in,' he says,' I can't get out at either end. I don't know what set me down in that Pawtucket horse-car and I don't know how I ever left that store or what became of it.' "

This case is by no means unique. It is given here in preference to others because the facts are vouched for by men of distinction in the scientific world.

Instances of this kind could be multiplied indefinitely. They illustrate the splitting-off from normal consciousness and from voluntary recall of a multitude of sensations which ought to be inseparably associated with the present.

These instances are exaggerated manifestations of that dissociation which is a characteristic of memory and normal mental activity. Such abnormal dissociation sometimes becomes habitual. It then results in that remarkable phenomenon, the subject of much recent investigation and discussion, the "secondary personality."

MULTIPLE PERSONALITIES

Chapter III

MULTIPLE PERSONALITIES

PHASES OF PERSONALITY

THE subject of secondary and multiple personalities includes many phenomena that were once regarded as mystifying and uncanny. Today the veil of occultism has been snatched away and we know the secondary personality for what it is, simply the symptom of a disordered mental mechanism, the personification of dissociation run wild.

The word "personality" has a variety of meanings. Commonly it denotes those individual characteristics by which one person is distinguished from another. Every personality in this sense is made up of changing materials. Socially, each one of us has almost as many different personalities as he has groups of acquaintances whose good opinion he values. To every such person he shows a different aspect of his nature.

The "social climber" does not appear among her "swagger" friends as she may show herself to the intimates of her household. The father is not the same man with his children as he may appear to be among the "good fellows" of his club. The merchant may be one man to his employees and another to his customers. The judge as an individual may feel profound compassion for the prisoner in the dock, yet as the minister phases of of justice he must mete out the penalty Personality that the law provides. Many a man would dread exposure to his business acquaintances of the character of his so-called "private life."

This disposition is not altogether a chameleon-like reflection of the characters of those about us. It is due in some degree at least to the love of approbation, the desire to so pattern our behavior as to simulate that picture of ourselves which we want those with whom we are in contact to carry in their minds.

In the phrases "primary personality," "secondary personality," and "multiple personality," as we shall use them, the term "personality" has no such significance as that we have been describing. In this connection it means, rather, a group of mental states bound together by a common element of memory.

PSYCHOLOGICAL ELEMENTS OF PERSONALITY

In normal life, all thoughts, all mental pictures, that come to us out of the past, are recognized by consciousness as part of our past. They do not come to us as new or strange. We know them for what they are, a part of ourselves.

All our conscious mental states, past and present, are therefore normally linked together by a mental sense of recognition not only as to their individual elements but as to each other. They merge into a flowing stream of consciousness.

Memory's recognition of the past as past thus unifies all conscious experience and enables us to think of ourselves as one individual or being.

HOW THE PERSONALITY MAY BE DISINTEGRATED

The man we were yesterday was but another manifestation of the man that we are today. And, in normal life, each person has normally but one "personality." There are, however, abnormal conditions in which one or more groups of mental states become split off from the others with no power of recognition or recall on the part of memory to bridge the gap.

A characteristic type of abnormal dissociation is that mental ailment known as functional amnesia, or forgetfulness, by which, as we have seen, a long period of time or an epoch in a man's life is blotted from his memory, is so dissociated from the stream of Personality consciousness that he is neither able to recall it nor to recognize it as belonging to his past. Another is the paralysis of anesthesia shown in cases of hysteria.

In the former type, the dissociation might be said to be a dissociation of conscious experiences, since it amounted to a setting off to one side of a vast number of experiences of which the individual was conscious at the time that they occurred but which by this dissociative process have become detached from his normal personality. In the latter type, the type of anesthesia, dissociation takes place simultaneously with the experience itself, so that the individual never at any time becomes conscious of it.

It is important to bear in mind that dissociation is a normal function of the mind, and, as a selective agency complementary to attention, enables the individual to adapt himself to the incessant changes of environment. It is only when the activity of this dissociating mechanism becomes enormously exaggerated or deranged that it is properly termed abnormal. That such disturbances are purely functional and indicate no brain defect is demonstrated by the cases cited in our last chapter evidencing the fact that these dissociations can be produced and removed by hypnotic suggestion. Obviously, a suggested idea could not be accepted and acted upon, if there was not a normal bodily mechanism.

SECONDARY PERSONALITIES

In the examples of abnormal dissociation we have thus far considered, the process has never gone beyond the failure to perceive or the inability to recall certain necessary sensory experiences. Such abnormal dissociations may, however, become so complete that the unperceived or lost experiences assume a systematic or organized form. We then have the phenomenon of abnormal life known as " secondary personality." By this is meant a separate group of mental states contemporaneous with the primary personality, but not connected with it by any power of conscious recollection.

"Secondary Personalities" have all the reality of another person with distinct traits and peculiarities inhabiting the body con- temporaneously with the true owner. Each group of mental states, each form of consciousness, has its own individuality and its own memory, but knows nothing of the existence of the other except through information gathered from outside sources. Illustrations will make this clear.

THE CASE OF, 'MADAME B'

One of the most famous cases of this sort is that of Madame B., of which Professor Janet's study and account has become historic. In this case the dissociation of mental states developed three distinct personalities, which are best described in Professor Janet's own words, as recorded by Mr. F. W. H. Myers:

"In these researches Mme. B., in her everyday condition is known by the name of Leonie. In the hypnotic trance she has chosen for herself the name of Leontine, which thus represents her secondary personality. Behind these two, this triple personality is completed by a mysterious Leonore, who may for the present be taken as nonexistent. A post-hypnotic suggestion was given to Leontine, that is to say, Leonie was hypnotized and straightway became Leontine, and Leontine was told by Prof. Janet that after the trance was over, and Leonie had resumed her ordinary life, she, Leontine, was to take off her apron — the joint apron of Leonie and Leontine — and then to tie it on again. The trance was stopped, Leonie was awakened, and conducted Prof. Janet to the door, talking with her usual respectful gravity on ordinary topics. Meantime, her hands— the joint hands of Leonie and Leontine — untied her apron, the joint apron, and took it off. Prof. Janet called Leonie's attention to the loosened apron. Why, my apron is coming off I' Leonie exclaimed, and, with full consciousness and intention, she tied it on again.

She then continued to talk, and for her — Leonie — the incident was over. The apron, she supposed, had somehow come untied, and she had retied it. This, however, was not enough for Leontine. At Leontine's prompting, the joint hands again began their work, and the apron was taken off again and again replaced, this time without Leonie's attention having been directed to the matter at all.

Next day Prof. Janet hypnotized Leonie again, and presently Leontine, as usual, assumed control of the joint personality. 'Well,' she said, 'I did what you told me yesterday! How stupid the other one looked ' — Leontine always calls Leonie 'the other one' — 'while I took her apron off! Why did you tell her that her apron was falling off? I was obliged to begin the job over again.'

"Thus far we have dealt with a secondary personality summoned into being, so to say, by our own experiments, and taking its orders entirely from us. It seems, however, that when once set up, this new personality can occasionally assume the initiative, and can say; what it wants to say without any prompting. This is curiously illustrated by what may be termed a conjoint epistle addressed to Prof. Janet by Mme. B. and her secondary personality, Leontine. She had left Havre more than two months when I received from her a very curious letter. On the first page was a curious note written in a serious and respectful style. She was unwell, she said, worse on some days than on others, and she signed her true name, Mme. B. But over the page began another letter in quite a different style, and which I may quote as a curiosity. *My dear good sir, I must tell you that B. really, really makes me suffer very much; she cannot sleep, she spits blood, she hurts me; I am going to demolish her, she bores me, I am ill also, this is from your devoted Leontine.' When Mme. B. returned to Havre I naturally questioned her about this singular missive. She remembered the first letter. I at first thought that there must have been an attack of spontaneous somnambulism between the moment when she finished the first letter and the moment when she closed the envelope. But afterwards these unconscious, spontaneous letters became common, and I was better able to study their mode of production. I was fortunately able to watch Mme. B. on one occasion while she went through this curious performance. She was seated at a table, and held in her left hand the piece of knitting at which she had been working. Her face was calm, her eyes looked into space with a certain fixity, but she was not cataleptic, for she was humming a rustic air; her right hand wrote quickly, and, as it were, surreptitiously. I removed the paper without her noticing me, and then spoke to her; she turned around, wide awake, but surprised to see me, for in her state of distraction she had not noticed my approach. Of the letter which she was writing she knew nothing whatever.

"Leontine's independent action is not entirely confined to writing letters. She observed (apparently) Leonore. And observe that just as Leontine can sometimes by her own motion and without suggestion write a letter during Leonie's state and give advice which Leonie might do well to follow, so also Leonore can occasionally intervene of her own motion during Leontine's dominance and give advice which Leontine might with advantage obey.

"The spontaneous acts of the unconscious self,' says M. Janet, here meaning by *l'inconscient* the entity to which he has given the name of Leonore, ' may also assume a very reasonable form, a form which, were it better understood, might perhaps serve to explain certain cases of insanity. Mme. B. during her somnambulism (i. e. Leontine) had had a sort of hysterical crisis; she was restless and noisy, and I could not calm her. Suddenly she stopped and said to me with terror, " Oh, who is talking to me like that? It frightens me." "No one is talking to you." " Yes! there on the left." And she got up and tried to open a wardrobe on her left hand, to see if someone was hidden there. "What is it that you hear?" I asked. "I hear on the left a voice which repeats, 'Enough! Enough! be quiet; you are a nuisance.'" Assuredly the voice which thus spoke was a reasonable one, for Leontine was insupportable; but I had suggested nothing of the kind, and had had no idea of inspiring a hallucination of hearing. Another day Leontine was quite calm, but obstinately refused to answer a question which I asked. Again she heard with terror the same voice to her left, saying: 'Come, be sensible; you must answer.' Thus the unconscious sometimes gave her excellent advice.

"And in effect, so soon as Leonore, in her turn, was summoned into communication, she accepted the responsibility of this counsel. 'What was it that happened,' asked M. Janet, 'when Leontine was so frightened?' 'Oh, nothing, it was I who told her to keep quiet; I saw she was annoying you; I don't know why she was so frightened.' "

"Just as Mme. B. was sent by passes into a state of lethargy from which she emerged as Leontine, so also Leontine in her turn was reduced by renewed passes to a state of lethargy from which she emerged no longer as Leontine, but as Leonore. This second awakening is slow and gradual, but the personality which emerges is in one most important point superior to either Leonie or Leontine. Alone among the subject's phases this phase possesses the memory of every phase. Leonore, like Leontine, "Madame B" knows the normal life of Leonie, but distinguishes herself from Leonie, in whom it must be said, these subjacent personalities appear to take little interest. But Leonore also remembers the life of Leontine, condemns her as noisy and frivolous, and is anxious not to be confounded with either."

You may wonder why we are leading you so far into abnormal and weird manifestations of mind. It is because of the light these abnormal phases shed upon the operations of the normal mind. You cannot, for example, have gone through these pages, and fail to realize that you may have distinct mental activities outside your consciousness.

THE MENTAL ATMOSPHERE

Chapter IV

THE MENTAL ATMOSPHERE

HIGH LIGHTS OF PERCEPTION

DISSOCIATION and its extreme result, forgetfulness, are not necessarily either abnormal or unhealthy. They are the mental processes that save us from a scattering of the mind that amounts to distraction.

Look out of the window. Imagine what meaningless confusion of light and shade and color you would have before you if some sense-impressions were not emphasized and others ignored. You can, if you try, distinguish every brick in the wall of the building across the way. Yet, thanks to dissociation, you get only the high lights, and what you really see is the building as an entirety.

ELEMENTS OF "THE GOOD STORY"

Some weeks ago I attended a dinner of the local Harvard Club. A spirit of good-fellowship reigned. The stories told, the jokes that were perpetrated, the songs that were sung, aroused the greatest enthusiasm and applause. Every number on the program was a "hit," and everyone had the best of "good times." The next day I tried to recount some of the funny stories I had heard, but to my surprise they not only fell flat but I myself was unable to discover anything particularly clever or witty in them. The fact is that the pleasure I had experienced in hearing them before was not due solely to the stories themselves; it was supplemented and re-enforced by other elements. The gayly decorated hall, the bright lights, the spirit of festivity and fun, all had contributed to the effect.

MENTAL FUSION

At any given moment we may be receiving simultaneous impressions through all the organs of sense, eyes, ears, nose, and so on, and at the same time be thinking of past experiences. These elements do not stand independent and isolated in consciousness. They all combine to produce a general effect that may be pleasurable or disagreeable.

SEEING THINGS AS WHOLES

The important phase of this from a practical standpoint is that in forming our first impression of things that we hear or feel or see we do not first sense individual elements and then put them together. We first receive a general impression of the whole, which we may later analyze into its component elements. And the extent of this analysis depends upon the frequency with which the experience occurs and upon the character of our interest.

To the infant mind a horse is a horse, with none of the radical distinctions and differences that are all-important to the judges in a horse-show. To the unimaginative mind, "a primrose by a river's brim a yellow primrose was to him, and it was nothing more." It revealed none of the marvels that would be so apparent to, say, the poet or the botanist.

THE COMMERCIAL ATMOSPHERE

So far as we are concerned, all things are interdependent. We see them only in their relationships. And these relationships constitute an integral part of the thing itself as we see it and know it. The clay that the sculptor works with is pure and clean, but, on the face and hands of the man who digs it, it is plain dirt. The food we eat may be ever so dainty, but it " soils " the napkin.

The fact that every object thus fuses with its environment and assumes the atmosphere of its surroundings is unconsciously recognized by most business men. It should be carefully considered by all.

Why does the bank in a great city house itself in an imposing masonry structure with walls four feet thick?

Is it only for greater security against fire and thieves? Is it not because of the confidence awakened in the depositors by this atmosphere of permanence and stability and vast resources?

THE "CHEAP-JOHN" STORE

Every store and office has an air of its own, and everything it offers, everything it does, is seen through this atmosphere. An acquaintance of mine wanted to buy a diamond. He had a friend who was a jeweler thoroughly honest and financially responsible. This jeweler offered him the kind of Stone he wanted at a net trade price. But the jeweler's store was of the "cheap-John" variety. Its windows were full of cheap novelties. And my acquaintance paid a much higher price for his diamond at the palatial and exclusive establishment across the way.

COLOR PSYCHOLOGY IN BUSINESS

The psychology of color plays an important part in salesmanship, and even in the wider conduct of affairs. The appeal, or lack of appeal, of colors to human sympathy, is well worth your careful attention. Your store may be situated equally as well as that of your competitor, yet he may outsell you simply because he knows how to make his place attractive by color-groupings. The customer will prefer his store to yours and never know why.

If you are a salesman you should realize that it is unwise to let a customer view one after another of a number of pieces of goods of practically the same color. Civilization has brought refinement of the color sense. A child will fill its arms with red roses. The woman of refined taste combines a single red rose with a spray of green leaves. Your buyer has a trained color sense, and you must make a subtle and discriminating appeal to it.

Be careful how you arrange your goods on shelves. Every color takes on to the eye a different hue when placed beside another color.

OFFICE FURNISHING
AND
STORE ARRANGEMENTS

Do not use a highly finished wood of definite color as a background for your pictures or your show-window. Everything in a color not complementary to such a background will suffer by contrast.

Furnish your library, office or director's room in a harmony of subdued tones, such as olives, browns or grays. They will make concentrated thinking easier.

The lawyer whose office is musty, dirty and poorly furnished may build up a good clientele, but he is working under a tremendous handicap. The doctor may be personally immaculate but no one will think so if he lives in an ill-kept house. You may be told that a certain store is the best place to purchase the article you need, but if you find that the whole establishment has a general air of shoddiness it will be hard to believe that the article it offers is of good quality. We cannot help feeling a greater respect for the firm that advertises in high-class magazines than for the one that employs handbills. We would certainly never patronize the manufacturer of food products who posted his advertisements on garbage boxes.

"A man is known by the company he keeps." This statement is just as true of things as it is of persons. The diamonds you have for sale may be of the first water and just what you represent them to be, but if the other things you have for sale are plated and pretentious shams I would be inclined to feel that your diamonds, too, were paste.

ESSENTIALS OF A GOOD PROSPECTUS

If you are selling stock in a new corporation, do not guarantee unusual profits unless you want your prospective purchaser to assume a skeptical attitude suspicious of fraud. Instead, simply array your facts in the most telling way you can and content yourself with the simple assurance that the profits will be "satisfactory." Your "prospect" will draw his own conclusions, and they, too, will be "satisfactory."

PSYCHOLOGY OF FIRST IMPRESSIONS

In these days business is done quickly and first impressions go a long way. The average man or woman does not take time for a careful critical analysis. He does not take a thing out of its environment, and set it apart for purposes of analytical study. Arguments are considered in conjunction with the personality and appearance of the man who makes them. Events are viewed in the light of surrounding circumstances. Objects are fused with the environment in which they are seen. If you have a store to arrange, or an advertisement to place, or salesmen to employ, or offices to furnish, it will pay you to consider the tendency of the human mind that we have been describing.

A SECOND ASPECT OF DISSOCIATION

Dissociation is the faculty that enables us to distinguish any object from its environment. Were it not for dissociation all sense-impressions would fuse into a blurred totality of confusion worse confounded. Each element would serve but to cloud and conceal all the others. Dissociation, when normal, is therefore an economizing mental process, a systematizing process, and it is controlled by the attention as fixed by desire, interest and will.

Attention and dissociation have their share in absolutely all mental activity. They operate not only to determine what department of subconsciousness the dissociated elements of experience shall fall into, but to determine also just what memories and just what present sense-impressions shall go to make up the present consciousness. We have been dealing with these discriminating tendencies so far as they affect our memory of past experience. We shall now discuss them as restricting the volume of the "stream " of consciousness.

DISSOCIATION AND THE ATTENTION

Chapter V

DISSOCIATION AND THE ATTENTION

RANGE OF ATTENTION ACTIVITY

THERE are two states of mind that peculiarly illustrate attention and dissociation as complementary processes. These two states of mind also offer interesting and indisputable evidence of the facts we have placed before you. One of these states of mind is the condition known as abstraction or absorption. The other is sleep. Both are simply degrees of limitation of the field of consciousness.

During our waking moments there are times when the dissociative faculty and conversely and consequently the attention as an emphasizing agency are more active than at other times. The degrees of this activity range from the most intense absorption in the business in hand to the sort of relaxed day-dreaming in which we allow our thoughts to wander here and there at the call of every association that incoming sense-impressions or a capricious reproduction of memory pictures may arouse. In each type all the senses may be awake, but in the former the attention, like a watchful sentinel, is alert to guard the mind of consciousness against all sensory impressions not provided with the countersign of relevancy, while in the latter the sentinel himself seems asleep and the dream palace of consciousness is open to every chance impression.

MEANING OF ABSENT-MINDEDNESS

The profound concentration of the attention, amounting to abstraction or absorption, is peculiarly characteristic of persons of unusual mental power.

As a matter of fact, it would seem that this phenomenon is in no sense an absence of mind, but is merely a concentration of the mental forces upon one subject to the exclusion of all else. Many anecdotes are related of Sir Isaac Newton, illustrating his so-called "absence of mind." On one occasion, when he was giving a dinner to some friends, he left the table to get them a bottle of wine. On his way to the cellar he became lost in reflection on some philosophic problem, forgot his errand and his company, and was soon hard at work in his study.

So Archimedes, when the Romans captured Syracuse, was so absorbed in his mathematical researches that he heard nothing of the noise and tumult that accompanied the taking of the city. Suddenly a soldier entered the philosopher's room and ordered him to go into the street. Archimedes, lost in thought, ignored the command, and the soldier in a rage plunged his sword into the philosopher's body.

It is told of the poet Lessing, that one evening upon arriving at his door he absent-mindedly inquired of the servant if her master was at home.

Receiving a negative reply, he said he would call again and walked away, Meaning of much to the servant's mystification.

Sir William Hamilton tells us that "the mathematician Vieta was sometimes so buried in meditation that for hours he bore more resemblance to a dead person than to a living one, and was then wholly unconscious of everything going on around him. On the day of his marriage, the great Buddaeus forgot everything in his philological speculations, and he was only awakened to the affairs of the external world by a tardy embassy from the marriage party, who found him absorbed in the composition of his 'Commentarii.'"

These classical instances have their counterparts to a greater or less degree in the lives of every one of us. Who has not at some time had the experience of suffering great pain from some accident or illness until so diverted by the humorous conversation of friends, or perhaps by some exasperating incident arousing his wrath, as to no longer be aware of even the slightest feeling of discomfort? Yet, when the incident came to an end, the pain would return. A soldier in the heat of battle has been known to hurl himself forward to the charge, knowing nothing of the fact that he had received his death-wound.

THE NEWS CENSORSHIP OF INTEREST

All these things show how, in the stress of profound mental activity or intense emotional excitement, the attention refuses to admit to consciousness sense-impressions which at another time would be of compelling interest. Under such circumstances, the senses continue mechanically to register impressions, and these impressions continue to be stored away in sub consciousness, perhaps to surprise us at some future day. Consciousness only is restricted to a narrow field.

The same principle is illustrated by the manner in which the mind disregards those familiar sense-impressions which by experience it knows to be of no interest. The business man in his downtown office does not even hear the roar of traffic on the street. But if he is compelled to return to work at his desk at night he will at once mark the unusual stillness. Throughout the day his senses had faithfully reported the street noise to his mind, but his discriminating attention had vigilantly diverted them from consciousness.

The countryman newly arrived in a great city gawks about, all eyes and ears. Almost every sense-impression means to him something new and strange or beautiful. Yet in a short time these things cease to interest him, until, in the midst of the city's turmoil, he is able to become absorbed in conversation with a friend.

The whispered sound of one's own name will attract his attention amid a babel of loud voices. The rumble of a passing street-car will be unperceived by one who will nevertheless be annoyed by the hum of a mosquito.

In all these cases a feeble sensation is allowed to become active in consciousness and is perceived with great clearness, while a throng of much stronger sensations occurring at the same time is forced to pass unnoticed. The hum of the mosquito is as nothing compared to the noise of the passing car, yet the car goes by unperceived.

Is it possible, then, that the light and sound vibrations coming from these external objects first awaken the senses, and that the senses then arouse the consciousness? Not at all: the senses and consciousness were all awake and active all the time, and they received these ether vibrations and disposed of them; hut that part of the mind called consciousness, and capable of looking in upon its own Operations, was concerned with only a small part of the news that was received.

SEEMING INTERMITTENCE
OF MIND LIFE

Mind, my mind and yours, seems to have an intermittent and interrupted existence. Sleep, fainting, and other so-called "unconscious" conditions occupy large periods of the mind life of each one of us. Does it follow that mind and mental activity have no existence during these periods?

As a matter of fact we know that the vital operations of the body are conducted with as much precision and efficiency during sleep as when we are fully awake. May we not suspect that other mental processes are carried on without our conscious knowledge during the "unconscious state"? May they not occur under these circumstances just as they took place without our of Mind Life knowledge in the examples of absent-mindedness, absorption and preoccupation that we have been considering? Certainly this might happen and none could be the wiser.

How often do we lie down for a nap of an afternoon and seem unable to fall asleep. After what seems but a few minutes of fitful dozing, we decide to give up trying to go to sleep, and are told, to our astonishment, that we have really been sleeping for an hour or two. Nothing but a look at the clock will afterwards convince us that we have really slept. Was the mind active during this unconscious interval as well as before and after? Certainly consciousness was interrupted, and if mental operations were performed, they were of a subconscious character. Let us see what the facts show.

PROOF OF MIND ACTIVITY DURING SLEEP

In the first place, whenever you fall asleep, there is always a first stage of "dozing off." Now, if you are gently aroused from this state, you will find that you are always in the middle of a dream, and you can trace its origin by a series of associations to your last conscious sense-impressions.

Again, suppose that after living in the country for some time, you move to the city and occupy a room in a downtown hotel. Your first night, with its multitude of unaccustomed noises, will bring you little repose. Yet, after a year of living in the same place, you will sleep as sweetly to the tune of street-cars, wagons and electric pianos as ever you did in the silence of the hills.

That the senses are less acute in sleep than when we are awake may be admitted. But when we are once asleep, they are just as sharp or just as torpid at the end of the year as they were on that first distressful night.

Why is it, then, that you were annoyed on the first night, but were not disturbed by the same noises some months later? The noises, the physical surroundings, are the same; the change, then, is not in the physical world, but is in your own mind and its activity.

SENSE DISCRIMINATION IN SLEEP

Clearly, the difference is identical with that we observed in the waking state as distinguishing the relaxed state of mind from that of preoccupation.

Suppose, for the sake of argument, that the mind does sleep with the body. Evidently the sleep of mind and of senses 'would he just as profound on the first night as on the last, and we would be unable to explain the first night's wakefulness.

It is plain, therefore, that the mind does not sleep like the body. Some element of the mind remains awake.

It is a discriminating element. On the first night this discriminating faculty of mind, made uneasy by unusual impressions, kept arousing consciousness to investigate; while on the last night, profiting by the lessons of experience, this discriminating faculty received these habitual and uninteresting Sense-impressions with tranquility and left in sleep consciousness to its slumber.

The same explanation accounts for the discrimination shown in sleep by those who nurse the sick and by the mothers of young babies. All other, even tumultuous, noises may be ignored, but let the patient groan or even breathe heavily, or let the infant whimper, or even stir restlessly in bed, and instantly the nurse or mother is fully awake.

THE PSYHOLOGY OF SLEEP

In the same way, many people have, to a remarkable degree, the faculty of measuring, during sleep, the flight of time. They are able to awaken at any given hour by simply making a firm resolve before retiring. Most persons habitually waken at the same time every morning. Indeed, the mind seems to measure the passage of time during sleep far more accurately than during the waking consciousness.

Is this possible unless there be mental activity during sleep? Does it not indicate that a watchful and discriminating faculty, call it attention, call it what you will, remains to guard the mind of consciousness from all disturbing sensory images excepting those which record the flight of time?

From the foregoing we must conclude that during sleep the senses deliver at least blurred impressions to some discriminating faculty of the mind; that this discriminating faculty of the mind passes judgment on these messages ; that it arouses us to full and wakeful consciousness only if the impressions be painful or surprising, or the sign of some external fact toward which the mind is in an attitude of expectant attention; that despite all this mental activity no one would contend that we are conscious during sleep, that sleep is, therefore, a state of subconscious mental activity.

THE EVER-WIDENING
MENTAL HORIZON

Here again, then, we have one more item added to the list of mental activities, energies and resources that are undreamed of in the average man's philosophy. There are, in fact, two features in all this that we would like to have stand out in your thought with, particular clearness. One is what must be for you the ever-widening horizon of your own mentality. The other is the process by which consciousness, the mind that governs our outward lives, is made up of such elements as attention selects for it.

Mark these important conclusions. Somehow and somewhere the mind retains the impress of all past experiences. Many are constantly being employed in our active, conscious mental life. Far the greater part are stored in the great reservoir of subconsciousness. Some are subject to voluntary recall; others are there, but are said to be " forgotten." They may be recalled by an exaltation of the memory, but for the moment are out of mind, because in the course of events our interests have changed and these so-called "forgotten" experiences are not related by any association of ideas with the subject of our present thought.

This sub consciousness is a reservoir of ideas, emotions and motor impulses bound into groups by similarities and contiguities of time, space and the like. These groups are in turn linked together by common elements into systems termed complexes. This sub consciousness is a reservoir of unfathomable depth; consciousness is but a passing ripple upon its surface.

Utilizing the lessons of experience

As our personal interests change with the exigencies of life, we correspondingly adjust the processes of attention and association on behalf of these interests. So it comes about that upon interest and attention depends the character of what we are able to recall, and upon the intensity and variety and complexity of our associations depends the quantity. Upon the reasonable cooperation of all these influences, together with the unfailing recognition of the past as past, depend the preservation of our normal mental life and our ability to appropriate and utilize to the highest degree for present needs the lessons of experience.

HOW TO DIRECT ONE'S THINKING

In all forms of "thinking," from the most listless reverie to the most intense volitional reasoning, association holds sway as the determining factor in the process. The only difference is that in reverie the attention swings freely from subject to subject at the instance of the passing whim, while in volitional reasoning to a desired conclusion, the will of the reasoner holds the attention steadfastly to those elements that it is desired to emphasize. The ones thus emphasized are in this way made the points of association, the common factors, with which the next idea must accord and to which it must relate. It thus appears that, by controlling the attention we can direct the associative processes and compel them to our will.

Attention is the holding in consciousness of a thought complex, either alone or in company with others.

Concentrated attention is exclusive attention to a single thought complex.

TWO KINDS OF CONCENTRATION

Concentration is an intense form of attention. If other subjects are allowed to enter consciousness, concentration may weaken into merely casual interest. The degree of concentration depends upon the extent to which all outside interests are inhibited.

Concentration of the attention may be continuous, as when you give exclusive attention for a time to the solution of some problem or the completion of some task. It may be intermittent, as when through several years you strive to accomplish some great financial undertaking. Consciousness is here repeatedly focused or concentrated upon related details of the same project.

To concentrate is to bar every interest but the one interest.

THE RULING PASSION

No man can continuously concentrate his attention for any great length of time. But remember this: If you are to have a successful business career, you must have some one great interest inspired by the idea of financial success, some ruling passion, that shall persistently hold sway.

INTEREST, ATTENTION AND BUSINESS

Chapter VI

INTEREST, ATTENTION AND BUSINESS

GENERAL LONGINGS AND SPECIFIC AIMS

IT IS not enough to have a mere general passion for success. Mere indefinite wishing for wealth will never get you anywhere. Besides this general passion you must have definite interests continually renewed. You must give the mind something specific and tangible and immediate to work upon. You must incessantly add new details. Otherwise interest, attention and activity will wane.

HOW TO MAINTAIN THE OUTPUT

Your biggest problem is how to keep your efficient output of mental energy at a high level. The solution lies in maintaining interest.

This is true whatever your business relationship. If you are an employer, you must continually devise new ways of renewing the interest of your men and inspiring them to concentrate their attention upon your business.

WHAT THE EMPLOYER MUST DO

You cannot put a young man into an office with monotonous routine duties to perform and expect him to take the interest that you take in your business. You must make his work interesting for him. You must give him a game to play, not expect him to put all his energy into playing your game.

It is no answer to say that the young man knew what the position meant before he took it. It is not a question of merely satisfying his craving for excitement in his work. It is a question of making his work interesting to him so that he will give it the best there is in him. It is not a question of any particular individual, because it is a question that must arise with every man who takes the "job."

There is no law compelling you to commend a man for special services he may render. Doubtless absolute devotion to your interests is what you pay him for. But if you take this attitude you will get just what you pay for — an automaton in the place where a live man ought to be.

REWARDS, COMMENDATIONS, COMPETITIONS

Appeal to the self-interest of your employees, arouse their living enthusiasm, concentrate their minds on your work with rewards, commendations, competitions, and ingenious devices calling forth a fresh play of forces, and you will get their best service and be following the policy of greatest business success.

If you are an employee, view the subject from its reverse side. You must bear in mind that your chances of advancement depend upon your concentration of interest and attention, and you must continually search your work for new sources of interest. You cannot work for a man, day in and day out, in the same old spiritless, automatic way, and expect your employer to shower you with opportunities and rejoice when your payday comes around.

THE MAN AT THE DOOR

Lose your interest in your employer's business, and a hundred men of equal ability are hammering at the door to take your place. You cannot succeed if your interest fails.

Keep your interest alive by trying to discover new things in old surroundings, new aspects to everyday tasks. The world was old when Columbus discovered America. You, too, may make. new discoveries in every department of your work. And always bear in mind that you are putting forth this added effort for the sole purpose of finding fresh sources of interest, as a means to greater concentration of attention on your work, the secret of individual efficiency and of your personal success.

WHAT THE EMPLOYEE MUST DO

Some men are interested in everything except the thing they are paid to think about. In consequence they are deaf, dumb and blind to all that concerns their business.

Others are so absorbed in their work that in all things relating to it they can "hear flies walking on the ceiling" and see the working of your brain-cells when you think.

Be alive, be alert, and the way to acquire these qualities is by habitually investigating the details of your business for the simple sake of finding new sources of interest.

FOUR INJUNCTIONS
FOR BUSINESS CONDUCT

Take the following four injunctions and make them working principles of conduct in your business.

1. Determine each morning upon the one definite thing worthwhile that you want most or all to do or to obtain that day. The being or doing or getting of anything worthwhile can come only as a result of an overmastering desire.

2. Do not admit the possibility of your own inability or defeat. It is the state of your own mind that makes for success or failure. Feel assured of your ability to do things, and you can go out among men and win them to your way.

3. Keep your attention riveted on the thing you want and your own ability to compass it.

4. Act promptly in the line of your desire.

Follow these rules and you will acquire the habit of concentration, the never-say-die spirit, the faculty of pushing ahead when the case seems hopeless, the courage, the tenacity, the resourcefulness that are indispensable to success.